honey-hearted

Taylor Byers-Chism

BookLeaf Publishing

India | USA | UK

Presentation by *BookLeaf Publishing*

Web: www.bookleafpub.com

E-mail: info@bookleafpub.com

ISBN: 9789363302198

First edition 2024

For Stevie, Jacob, and my entire family: Thank you for always believing in me, even when I didn't. I love you.

PREFACE

"Tell me, what is it you plan to do with your one wild and precious life?" -Mary Oliver

pat#way

I hope one day,
if we were to
ever cross paths,
you would not
spend a second filled with
dread.

Heart,
openly bleeding,
I root for you.

I don't even care if
you root for me,
too.

found@tional

Please be careful
not to build
sandcastles

with people unwilling
to close their fingers.

The small glass
granules
of your heart
will never catch hold.

They will beg for
each and every
grain.

And in the end,
it will only ever
be you

that is empty.

-betwe3n-

I think that's the difference
between
you and me.

Despite the hurt,
I never wanted to
hurt you
too.

I did not mean to
stick my fingers
deep into
your open wounds.

Flesh torn,
in need of
heavy stitches.

My heart accidentally
bleeding
substantially onto yours.

Hands covering
your wounds,
unable to stop the flow.
I only wanted to hold you

as we bled out silently
together.

canva$

Beautiful, tiny fingers
wrapped around my pinky;
heartbeats syncing.

Sore layers of flesh
sit atop the empty cavern of my body
that was once your protection.

Now that you are out in the world,
I feel unable to shelter you as I once did,
to shield you from harm.

Everything about you seems delicate:
soft, squishy, and malleable.

A single prick or fall could be the end.

I don't know if I'm cut out for this –
being a safety net for such a fragile being.

As months pass,
you gain head control,
start rolling over,
and then you walk!

Oh, but to see you grow –

it is but such a beautiful thing.

Days count on and
fears ease as you grow bravely.

Suddenly, transformed
into a wild and courageous
YOU.

My body, no longer an empty cavern
but a cozy home, covered in scar tissue
and jammy fingerprints.
 A canvas of love.

Beautiful, squishy, little thing
how unaware you are that
I am learning too.

dandelion

People are creatures
of repetition;
moving without thought.

Never simply floating
like the small
delicate seeds on a
dandelion.

Like water,
humans ebb and flow.
Ultimately
ending up in the same place.

But why is it
that you feel like a
dandelion seed?

Always searching for
a safe place to land.

Drifting and soaring,
waiting for the most
important parts
to spread.

{ink}

I am like you,
you are like me,
too.

Yet in a room,
of just us two,

misfiring
neural pathways
cannot link.

And I can only
speak in
ink.

My heart says,
"Reach out,
you are not alone."

And yet
my mouth
stays
silent.

It is only my
fingers that

ever
speak.

How can I
let my
mouth bleed
out
when the only thing that
can escape is
this
thick black ink?

R0ck T0wërs

I fell in love with you on the beach that day,
Knees covered in sand,
Creating rock towers silently.
I remember the look in your eyes as we
tossed pebbles and exchanged glances.
How your lips curled around unspoken words
and a half-soaked cigarette.

I fell in love with you in the mornings
Filled with stale coffee and lingering
conversations.
That goofy laugh that could be heard for miles
Along that sandy shoreline.
My awkward knobby knees gently brushing
against yours.

I fell in love with you at the airport
When both of our bodies couldn't stop shaking
and eyes that couldn't stop crying.
The haunting fear of never seeing you again
causing such a heavy sorrowful goodbye.

I fell in love with you the moment that I saw
you.
I knew you in another world,
Another lifetime.

Our souls forever intertwined;
Healing a deeply rooted loneliness that always
Lingered within mine.

I STILL fall in love with you,
Every day that I come through the door.
Exhausted and full of rage from wearing an
invisible mask that no one understands,
You let me know that you do.
In unspoken words, you let me know that
Neither of us are alone.

A decade later, I am perpetually still falling in
love with you.

(stardust)

You cannot comprehend
how incredibly hard
it has been to try and be
normal.

The amount of time
spent,
practicing conversations
and making sure that
my face didn't have subtitles.

Just to be met with
rude comments and unwanted advances.
Most of which smudgy rose colored
glasses so easily
disguised.

What would it take for you to
understand
that we are
both made from the same
stardust?

Some of us
are just perpetually
imploding internally.

jdc

How could I explain
to you that
I was just an old oak tree
with mangled roots
obstructing the foundation
of someone else's
home?

And how is it that,
even now,
you still see
me as
the effervescent soap-film
that dances on the breath
of our daughter's
whispered wishes?

Together,
rooted and floating,
simultaneously;
infinitely.

h0ney-he@rted

I am guilty of one thing,

I wanted a heart so full
of amber honey-love,

a heart,
so overrun with warm gooey goodness,
that it could not be contained
in my
plastic bear chest.

But instead,
I let my love
get all over your hands.

Leaving sticky, dirty fingerprints
behind.

All that
I wanted was for my heart to
feel like childhood
 to you.

But instead, it just left
 a giant mess
for me to clean.

b100d

We share the same blood.
And between the two of us,
it runs thin.

Air thin.

I just wanted you to see
that despite it all
we share the same
heart.

And that they beat
with
the same blood.

Yet,
In this moment,
water
holds more weight than
air-thin blood.

m!nd

Lilac petals and pie crusts
litter my childhood memories.

Moth balls and creaky basement steps
lead to the depths of my heart.

I see you in gardens,
scattering eggshells of hope
on your tomato dreams.

You are always there in the
back of my mind,
coaching me on how to hold
my knitting needles.

I can still feel your
work-worn hands on my back
reassuring me as I fall asleep.

Sewing machines, bubbly sourdough,
and mason jar dreams keep me close to you.

I hear you in my mother's laugh
Over the phone;
Reminders that we're never truly alone.
Your roses would bloom just in time

for my visits in early June.
Even when your mind wanders
to the brink of forgetting,
you are never very far from me.

I see little bits of you in everything.

sh!pwrecked

Grief,
they say,
comes in waves.

Today,
I am a
human shipwreck.

Every wave,
wreaking havoc on
my rotten soggy floorboards.

Wreckaged arms
outstretched
for tiny shorelined
fingers.

A small lighthouse body
beaconing me
to separate
from the swell of the ocean.

Yet
My anchor
too weak to
not disintegrate.

I just wanted to make it home.

eclect!c sunshine

I wish you could feel
the electricity that is
my soul.

Encompassed in
skin
framed in
bones.

9 million volts
of eclectic sunshine
straight
to your heart.

zap.

@nonymous

I bet you weren't aware
of the implications
that letting those vile
words slip
would have on me.

The words of our childhood,
once sweet and kind,
turned to splintered glass with age.

Lodging themselves further into the
recesses of my gummy bear heart

And if you were aware,
would you take it back?

I stayed up every night,
contemplating if I should
follow your advice and say
a final goodbye.

I felt utterly alone;
mascara streaked down
my face and pillowcase.
Filled with questions that
would haunt me for years.

I realized that you
didn't deserve to win.

Despite your words echoing
through the halls of my mind,
disrupting every ounce of peace,
and making me doubt my worth,
I found strength.

No one deserves to feel
unworthy of their life.

Not even you.

I hope you find resilience
in your own battle too.

place

I was not prepared
to have to
hold a place in my heart
for the people whom
have hurt me.

A safe place of mutual
 understanding
that it was never
about my life.

This place has a sign
out front that reads,
"It's okay, you are
always
welcomed here.

My heart forgives you.
Come in."

our0boros

If the eyes are the window to the soul,
why do mine resemble coiled-up snakes?

Light blue, with scaly specks,
waiting to unfurl and shake their rattle.

Little misunderstood ouroboros,
perpetuating unity
in a cycle of
destruction and re-creation.

Perhaps never meant to be found in,
on a cyclical path of their own.

<light>

All my life, I was convinced
I was the shipwreck.

Yet here I stand on the shore,
 beckoning lost ships home,
guarding the secrets of the waves,
and witnessing the sun
fall in love with the skyline every night.

I hear the seagulls cry for the freedom
 I once sought and remember
the storms that nearly ripped me apart.

The waves that tried to drown my soul
now give me strength,
and I found resilience in the tides.

A pillar of strength,
I am the keeper of the night,
showing others the way to the light.

Beaconing you safely back home.